Executor's Function Guide

(revised 2008)

Procedures

Explanations

Documentation Required

Sample letters to aid with your correspondence to various agencies and Government bodies, including pension boards.

revised March 2008   Author: Stephen Paul Tolmie

AuthorHouse™
1663 Liberty Drive
Bloomington, IN 47403
www.authorhouse.com
Phone: 1 (800) 839-8640

Published by AuthorHouse 04/20/2015

ISBN: 978-1-4343-9951-9 (sc)
ISBN: 978-1-4678-3559-6 (e)

Print information available on the last page.

This book is printed on acid-free paper.

<u>Dedication</u>

I would like to dedicate this book to my parents, William Donald Tolmie and Nellie Irene Tolmie. This couple came through the depression, the second world war, found each other, married and raised two children, worked through life's hard knocks and have recently celebrated sixty two years of marriage.

I believe that overall, my life was enriched having this wonderful couple as my parents.

<u>Note of Appreciation</u>

I wish to express a heartfelt thank you to
Dennis Goddard, owner of Goddard Design,
for his knowledge, his talent and his artistic skills
as displayed in the eye catching cover of my book.

I was fortunate to have had his talent at a time
when I needed direction for my book's cover design.

Thank you Dennis.

__Acknowledgements__

In undertaking the writing of this book,
I am continuing to face the everyday challenges
of dealing with the death of my partner-in-life.
I know full well that this can only be accomplished
with the help of many good friends.
I am especially grateful to Marion Broadfoot,
a special friend who helped me in the preparation of
readying this book for publication.

I would also like to recognize Patricia Ann Dean
for her assistance in adding the inserts to my
book and organizing the material in an orderly fashion.
She also did additional typing to further enhance
the information that I wanted to present.
Thank you for all you have done for me, and thank you
all from who will reap the benefits of this workbook.
Your time, energy and professionalism have been
well spent and greatly appreciated.

Table of Contents

Healing and Closure

As a suggestion and as help in the healing and closure process, I found putting a pen to paper and expressing my feelings was easier than speaking to a family member, a friend or a consultant.

With regard to this, I wrote a poem in an effort to find my own inner strength ... my heart and soul ... the very essence of WHO I am, of where I am at this stage in my life, and where I intend to go from here on.

Will You Remember Me

You came into my world when there was pain and sorrow.
You intensely listened. You seemed to care.
You stated your opinion, to always be there.
We shared good times and bad.
We drifted emotionally apart,
Then like a tide, returning, we slowly touched again.

Our emotions still intact, we seemed very cautious.
We seemed unprepared to touch one another's life,
But we felt a bond emerging,
a desire beginning to grow.

Will our lives connect, or strictly just be friends?
Will another tide take you from me?
Will my world end?
Will pain and sorrow once again appear
to fill my life's existence?
Will emotions never end?

Written by Stephen Paul Tolmie
December 19, 2004

Do You Need Estate Planning

Questions you need to ask yourself ...

1. What is Estate Planning?

2. What is involved in Estate Planning?

3. Who needs Estate Planning?

4. What is included in my assets?

5. What is a Will?

6. What is "Revocable Living Trust"?

7. What is Probate?

8. To whom should I leave my assets?

9. Whom should I name as my Executor or Trustee?

10. How should I provide for my minor children?

11. When does Estate Planning involve Tax Planning?

12. How does the way in which I hold title make a difference?

13. What are other methods of leaving property?

14. What if I become unable to care for myself?

15. Who should help me with my Estate Planning documents?

16. How do I find a qualified Lawyer?

17. Should I become aware of someone who is a "promoter" of Financial and Estate Planning services?

18. What are the costs involved in Estate Planning?

The Power of Attorney

What is the significance of this statement?

What does it entail?

The reality of this statement means you are giving someone the **"POWER TO SIGN YOUR NAME"**.

They can sell your home. They can enter you into debt and they can sell all of your assets. This could in reality be giving away all of your assets and your identity. As a person of self worth this is not something that you should jump into quickly without realizing how it works and what you may be getting into.

A Continuing Power of Attorney for Property (as it is called in Ontario) is a legal document. It gives a person or persons of a grantor's choice, the ability to manage his affairs, so long as he was competent and capable when he granted this authority. The word "continuing" is used because the document stays in force after the person who gave it (the Grantor) is no longer capable.

There is a sister document which relates to personal care. In Ontario, this is called the "Power of Attorney for Personal Care." For this document one chooses one or more capable people to make medical and personal health decisions on his or her behalf. These decisions would be made only if you are incapable of doing so.

The document "Power of Attorney for Personal Care" is often confused or used interchangeably with what has been commonly known as the "Living Will". A Living Will itemizes a capable person's instructions for medical intervention if he or she becomes incapable.

In a Living Will you may state whether or not you want to be resuscitated or have a breathing tube inserted. The Living Will is an expression of desired options for medical response. It does not appoint someone to act on your behalf.

In Ontario, the Living Will is incorporated into the Power of Attorney for Personal Care, while in other jurisdictions, it may operate as a "stand alone" document.

The Continuing Power of Attorney for Property in Ontario is called an "Enduring Power of Attorney." It is referred to as a "Mandate" in Quebec. The Power of Attorney for Personal Care in Ontario is known in other provinces as a "Health Care Directive" or "Personal Directive".

The Continuing Power of Attorney for Property and its counterparts across the country have inherent risks, but if structured and executed in a thoughtful manner, the document can operate as an effective financial and personal planning tool.

As you can readily see, it is imperative that good open and honest conversation with family members be held in order to ensure there will be a swift and smooth transaction of your wishes. A similar process should be carried out when dealing with a lawyer. He needs to have all the I's dotted and the T's crossed to ensure that your wishes are carried out in a timely desired fashion.

Your decision to give the power of attorney to a person should be with someone you know. Someone who you feel shares your values, and beliefs. This person is someone you know will be strong enough in his or her own beliefs: someone who can give a logical explanation as to how the process will be done.

When giving this power of attorney to someone for your personal care you may find the selection of a person for that job much tougher. It is crucial to find the right person to fulfill your medical wishes. Again this person must have your beliefs, both religious and moral, as they may need to make a life and death decision especially if you are at any time placed on life support due to a life-threatening situation. If they do not have your beliefs you need to know that they will be able to respect your wishes and make the decision you have chosen.

Power of Attorney for Personal Care not only includes the type of care (institutional or home care) but also includes nutrition, hygiene and safety issues. When it comes to granting a Power of Attorney for Personal Care, the person who handles financial affairs may not necessarily be the best candidate.

An all-important back up plan should be in place for the person assigned with the Power of Attorney. What if the person who is your first choice should become incapacitated or dies? Who then would be your second or third choice? It would not hurt to approach these potential choices to see if they would undertake this responsibility. This is not a time to "assume" anything. You may feel they would be honored to take on the responsibility but in fact it may impose a burden on them... something they may not want to undertake.

Be sure to have a Continuing Power of Attorney in place. This can be part of one's personal financial planning. Having this document in place will ensure that your assets will not fall under government control also known as The Public Guardianship.

The Public Guardianship occurs when an agency takes care of the property, financial affairs and physical needs of an older adult who is not mentally capable of making decisions.

This Public Guardian and Trustee may not be aware of your wishes regarding the dispersement of your assets. They may not be aware of your personal care wishes unless they take the time to read your documents, and just how likely is that to happen? Their track record has been known not to be very good at the best of times.

Furthermore, Canadian studies have found that financial abuse is the most commonly reported form of abuse experienced by older people. Relatives are often front and center in such situations. There have been cases where sons and daughters have bought cottages and paid off car loans and mortgages with the Power of Attorney that gives them access to a parent's savings.

A safeguard against abuse includes having two signatures on all cheques and other documents and daily withdrawal limits on bank accounts. Having a reporting system in place is a necessity and ensures one's peace of mind.

If you witness financial abuse of an incapacitated friend or relative, there is a solution. For a fee, you can go to court to obtain a guardianship order for the incapacitated person. This guardian order would trump the Power of Attorney.

My final thoughts are to remind you to" **think before you act".** In other words do your homework. Choose carefully as to whom you wish to appoint as your Power of Attorney. Be sure to ask the appropriate questions. Weigh their answers. Then, finalize your thoughts. Be sure the persons you choose are in harmony with your wishes.

For those of you who wish further information or help with financial planning, you may download free information from the web onto your computer, from "The Canadian Financial Security" program. From their site, financial and legal documents are free and financial information is available from their site at http://www.truehelpfinancial.com . When you join the program, you will receive free access to books and documents. They simply ask you to complete a short (2 – 3 minutes) survey when you join. There is no financial cost for membership.

Distribution of Your Money

There is no limit to the amount of cash gifts you can give in a year, and the best part is that it is tax-free. You can save taxes by placing funds into your beneficiary's hands while you are alive. This method will keep the money out of your estate and therefore prevent the funds going to the tax department.

It is wise to consider this method of distributing your funds as when you die, all investments are considered to be "sold". If there is a large amount of funds the taxes will be at a higher marginal rate.

The old phrase, "save some for a rainy day" comes to mind here. Never give too much of your acquired wealth to your beneficiaries as you may require extra finances for you and your spouse down the road. Be aware the average life expectancy is on the rise and you may need to hold onto enough monies to cover future extended health care and living costs.

It is always important to seek professional financial assistance to help you understand the tax ramifications that could affect your money, property or other investments. An advisor could also supply you with other information such as capital gains tax and dispersement fees that you may not have had knowledge of when setting up your estate.

Are you able to disinherit one of your children? The only basis for challenging disinheritance is if the child was a dependant and was receiving support from their parents.

Some people like to leave money to charities. There are a number of ways to do this. One way is to name a charity directly as a beneficiary of a RRSP or RRIF or of a life insurance policy. Again, a professional financial advisor can best direct you on the disposition of your assets. His or her skills will help eliminate probate fees and claims to creditors.

Other ways to eliminate probate fees include:

- Consider a charitable annuity if over 70 years of age

- Set up a family foundation (start up costs 0f $5000 - $25000 may be involved)

- Consider an endowment fund with a community foundation. (give minimum donations of $20,000 - $25,000 and dispense at least 3.5% of the invested assets each year.

Wills

Law fact: A person that passes with a will is said to be "testate" and is referred to as a "Testator". A person without a will has passed "intestate". A Will refers to a legal document that details your wishes for how your assets will be distributed at the time of your passing. A common misconception is that only those that are wealthy need Wills. This could not be farther from the truth, as a Will is recommended for everyone, especially those with children or other dependents. It should be noted that those who die without a Will in place, would have their assets distributed as defined by their state or province of residency law. This may or may not match your wishes. This makes your Will an important part of estate planning.

Since a Will can be a complicated legal document, it is generally recommended by most estate planners that a lawyer be consulted to assist in the preparation of the Will. Although Wills can be completed independently, often using software packages or predefined forms, it should be noted that these Wills may not cover many of the more complicated aspects of probate law. Of course, consulting with a lawyer to prepare your Will is the most costly option. Self-preparation can be done very inexpensively in many cases.

Typically, the legal requirements that must be met to make a Will legally binding include:

- The testator must be a legal adult, at least 18 years of age

- The testator must clearly mark himself as the creator of the Will

- The testator must revoke all previously made Wills (e.g. only the most recent Will be legally binding)

- The testator must demonstrate that creation of the Will is done freely and willingly and that the testator is of sound mind

- The testator must sign and date the Will (at the end of the document), usually in the presence of at least two witnesses who do not have an interest in the will.

Making Your Will Secure

It is imperative that you keep your Will up to date as events change in your life.

Some examples of changes that could occur are as follows:

- Buying a home and or a seasonal home

- Moving to another country or province

- Being married, divorced, or living with a new partner

- Having children, or acquiring step children

- Having the death occur of a person that is a beneficiary listed in your estate

- Buying an investment property

- Having your executor not be able to carry out their functions due to age or illness

- Anyone mentioned in your Will changes their name

The above examples automatically require that a change be made in your Will. I would suggest that as an aid you use this workbook or a Will kit to place your revisions in writing. It can also be used to express your ideas and wishes for dispersements of your estate.

Only a **lawyer** can legally draw up your Will and prevent you from making errors that could tie up your Will in a court of law. Your Will needs to be bulletproof in order to prevent speed bumps that may delay the people you love from receiving your assets the way you wished. A securely written Will can allow the dispursements to be made without a lengthy delay in a time that your family may require money. It also prevents the possibility of the Will being tied up in a costly court system.

<u>When to Seek Legal Advice</u>

- Need tax advice

- Have minor children

- Are in a second marriage

- Need advice about marriage contracts

- Have obligations to common law partners

- Need a Will with trusts to protect beneficiaries

- Live in assisted care or have been recently ill or hospitalized

- Have substantial investments, a business or a second home

A key point to be aware of is that any life insurance policies should be designated to go directly to your named beneficiary. Three good reasons for this are as follows.

- Your beneficiary may need the funds to pay for your funeral expense if not already paid for.

- Your family may need the capital to work with in order to cover unforeseen costs. (immediate cash flow).

- Probate costs can be reduced

Not wanting to assume anything at this point, it is very beneficial to have your assets (such as a home) **jointly owned** with your spouse. The surviving spouse will usually inherit this asset without probate problems.

When you own assets with your children or a third party, you risk loosing control of these assets due to disagreements between children, or your children's creditors may make a claim to your properties. Even a common law partner may have legal rights to share in your estate.

If there is a challenge to your Will or if someone sues your estate, all could be frozen until the lawsuit is finished. This scenario could delete your assets with all having been lost to the costs incurred in a lengthy court battle. Keep in mind that your Will may have been set up to look after minor children until they are of legal age and it is imperative that the funds be available for this to happen. Also it is wise to have more than one guardian set up to care for minor children in case there is an accident that may kill you, your wife and the original guardian listed.

Remember to review your Will each time your assets change, or your beneficiary's change. Your lawyer will need to document these changes in order to ensure that your wishes will be carried out. A properly thought out Will is an investment to protect your family and it can never be too costly.

In closing, a Will is the very essence of you and your wealth. You should pay to have a properly executed Will now, so that your appointed beneficiaries will receive what you wish them to have after your demise.

What is Probate?

As defined, Probate is "A sign of future occurrences".

Probate when required, is the process undertaken by the executor named in the Will. It begins with the executor itemizing the deceased's assets and ends with the Provincial Court providing the executor with the authority, (sometimes called "Letters Probate") to give instructions to the appropriate financial institutions.

The Federal Government also wants its share of taxes based on the deceased's taxable income in the year of death. It is the executor's duty to file a final tax return on the deceased's behalf. In essence, do your estate planning to minimize the smallest amount of personal income tax that your estate will have to pay to the government. As the saying goes" nothing is certain but death and taxes" and the government will be looking for that money.

Be well aware that taxes can be minimized when you name a beneficiary on your life insurance polices, pension plans, RRSP, RRIF etc. These assets are distributed outside of your Will and are not included in the calculation of your probate tax. Also, when assets are registered jointly with a spouse or common law partner, the assets remain with them on your death and again these assets are not included in the calculation of your probate tax.

Once a Will has been probated, third parties can be certain the executor has the legal authority to act on behalf of the estate.

A few more ideas you may find helpful in reducing the amount of taxes that will be payable to the government are as follows.

- Leave a spouse or partner (common-law or same-sex), registered assets and those assets, which have untaxed capital gains. Deferring the tax on these assets helps to preserve their value. As well, it may offer the opportunity for them to increase in value over time.

- Provide your executor(s) with discretionary powers, to make elections under the Income Tax Act that would be in the best interests of any estate beneficiaries that may not have existed at the time your Will was prepared.

- An accountant reviewing the final tax return may ensure no more tax is paid than necessary. Give your executor the authority to hire and pay for the services of a professional accountant. This money can be well spent.

- The executor can seek an advisor to help them decide if optional returns may be filed on behalf of the deceased. As many as three optional returns can be filed if applicable. Certain tax exemptions and credits can be used more than once thus saving taxes that need to be paid.

  "Optional" returns are:

  - Earned business income from a partnership or sole proprietorship with a year-end that was not December 31.

  - Income from a Testamentary Trust with a year-end that was not December 31.

  - "Rights and Things" that were due but not yet paid. "Rights and Things" could include vacation pay, salary, commission income and/or investment income.

Anyone with more than one residence needs to decide which one is their primary residence, as Capital Gains on a principal residence are exempt from tax.

When the spouse or partner in the household dies, the most immediate financial concern is, "Can I get my hands on enough money to buy the groceries?" Therefore it is a good idea to ensure that **all bank accounts be joint accounts** as this will enable your spouse or executor to have ready access to those funds. Cash flow will be important at this time and the accounts will not be frozen until after probate is carried out.

My closing thought is that you should always include yourself in your estate planning. It is your money; you made it, so enjoy it throughout your retirement. Always remember that you cannot take it with you.

General Information

IF YOU DIE WITHOUT A WILL, and you are married, what you leave behind does not automatically go to your spouse as many people think. Depending on the size of your estate, only a portion may be given to your spouse and the remainder may be divided among your children and your spouse. If you are not married, your estate usually goes to your parents or is divided among your brothers and sisters. A court will appoint an administrator who will usually receive compensation from the proceeds of the estate. Your assets may well be tied up "in Probate" for a long time and then may not be distributed as you might have wished. If your Will is not properly done, again, your possessions may be "tied up" in Probate and then given to someone that you may not have wished would receive them. This is not what you want to happen!

A simple Will can be filled out by you and will usually hold up quite well in court if such becomes necessary.

When your estate is simple, that is:

- When your assets are easily identified and your ownership of those assets is unquestionable

- When you don't own a lot of rental real estate unless it is properly jointly owned where you want the person with whom you share ownership to have full possession if you die

- When there is little likelihood of disputes over your estate

- When you're not second guessing yourself as you try to fill out your Will, then preparing your own Last Will and Testament can be done easily.

However, I believe that having a Will done by a good lawyer, at least in this country, is a bargain in most cases. If you have a sizable estate or any complications, I would encourage you to spend the few hundred dollars necessary and visit a qualified lawyer.

There are three estate-planning documents to address.
They are as follows:

- **Last Will and Testament**
- **Enduring Power of Attorney**
- **Living Will (also referred to as a "Health Care Directive")**

As there is some terminology used in Wills that not everyone is familiar with, let us first define some terms you may need to use.

BENEFICIARY: A person named in a Will, Trust, or Insurance Policy, etc. to receive assets or payments.

BEQUEATH: To give by means of a Will.

CLEARANCE CERTIFICATE: A certificate from the Income Tax Department confirming that all tax owing by the estate has been paid.

CODICIL: A written change to part of a Will that is not intended to cancel the whole Will.

ENDURING POWER OF ATTORNEY: A Power of Attorney that continues in effect after its maker loses mental capacity.

EXECUTOR: One who is appointed by a testator to carry out the terms of his/her Will.

EXECUTOR'S YEAR: The time assumed to be reasonable for an executor to finalize an estate.

EXECUTRIX: The feminine of "Executor". It is becoming less common in use, as the term "executor" is now acceptable for both male and female.

GUARDIAN: A person appointed in a Will to care for minor children. Also, a person appointed in a Living Will or by a court order to make health and physical care decisions for an adult who is unable to do so due to mental or physical disability.

INTESTATE: Dying without a Will.

JOINT WILLS: Wills that are identical and cannot be changed without the consent of both Will makers.

LAST WILL AND TESTAMENT: The most recent instructions left by a deceased as to the disposition of his/her property, which is everything that he/she owns including assets that may be owed to him/her.

LIVING WILL: (Also called Advance Health Care Directive, Health Care Directive, Personal Directive, Authorization to Give Medical Consent, Continuing Power of Attorney for Personal Care, or Representation Agreement for Health Care.); a document that appoints someone to make medical and health care decisions if the maker is unable to make such decisions due to a mental or physical incapacitation such as a coma, etc. This instrument should indicate what medical treatment you desire in the event that you are unable to communicate due to incapacitation.

PROBATE: Pertaining to making proof, especially legal proof, as of a Will. The processes of having a court certify that a Will is in fact the true last Will of the deceased.

PROBATE COURT: A court having jurisdiction of proving Wills.

PROCTOR: A lawyer, usually appointed or hired by an executor to help with the legal aspects in carrying out the terms of a Will.

PUBLIC TRUSTEE: A government official appointed under provincial jurisdiction to look after the affairs of those who have no one else to do so, either during their lifetime or after death.

TESTATE: Having made a Will before death.

Parts of a Will

- The **date** is extremely important, because this Will is going to invalidate previous Wills.

- You would usually write a statement **revoking any previous** Wills.

- A direction is usually given, to **pay** for your "just debts, funeral expenses and any expenses arising from the administration" of your Will.

- You **appoint an executor** of your estate.

- You clearly identify and **bequeath your belongings** to whom you choose.

- If you have minor children you may appoint a **guardian** in your Will.

- You may wish to set up a **trust** or trusts for any minor children or for any other person or cause that you may want to provide continued support for after your death.

- Your Will **must** be witnessed by **two** people, who must both be present together when you sign the Will.

- **You** must sign your Will in the **presence** of the two witnesses, and **in the Province of Quebec** both you and the two witnesses must **initial each page.** This is not mandatory in the rest of Canada but it is always a good idea to have all pages initialed even if it is not a requirement.

Property Ownership

It can be very helpful in preparing to transfer the things you own to others, to have a clear understanding of how the law sees property ownership. Three types of ownership are as follows:

• Joint Assets With The Right Of Survivorship

• Designated Beneficiary Assets

• Everything else

Understanding these terms and the rights that go with them may motivate you to change how you own some things before you die, so when you do die, your property may go to whom you wish in a more expedient manner.

JOINT OWNERSHIP WITH THE RIGHTS OF SURVIVORSHIP, often called "joint tenancy" when referring to a house, means that each of the named individuals simultaneously owns the entire asset. So, when one joint owner dies, the surviving owner already owns the entire asset no matter what a Will might say. This is the best way to own a house or other property, a bank account (joint account), investments, etc., in the case of a secure married couple when there are no complications. This method of ownership also works well and is very commonly used where there is an aging parent and assets are owned jointly between a parent and a trusted adult child. This is, by far, the best way to pass on assets without the complications of Probate, etc. as long as there is a great degree of trust and integrity.

DESIGNATED BENEFICIARY ASSETS are things like life insurance policies, RRSP's, RRIF's, LIRA's, pensions, etc. that pass to a nominated survivor at your death regardless of what you may say in your Will.

EVERYTHING ELSE you own is really what you are going to deal with in your Will. Whether it is money, investments, a coin collection, your favorite vase, or your clothing, it is yours to give to whomever you wish, and such can happen as long as your wishes are clearly known.

Witnesses

A legally acceptable Will must be witnessed by two people. The two witnesses must be present with you, together when you sign the document. The witnesses can be anyone who has reached the age of majority, even a close relative. A witness cannot be a beneficiary of anything in the Will. Do not use anyone as a witness who may wish to purchase anything from your estate.

If a Will must be "probated", that is proved by use of the courts, at least one of the witnesses will be asked to be present at that time. Because of this, it is important, if you move to another province, to update your Will accordingly, otherwise, it becomes difficult and slow to finalize your last wishes.

Revoking a Will

There are three ways to revoke or cancel a Will:

- destroy it
- make a new one
- get married

Duties of an Executor

Just what does it mean to be an executor? A simple explanation is that he or she has been named in a Will to handle an estate when someone dies.

The size and the many aspects of an estate especially as to how well the person's affairs are in order, can prove to be easy, or can become a difficult and time consuming process for the executor.

Any person who has been asked to take on this task should be well aware as to what it means and just what is involved.

Possible duties of an executor:

- Find, read and interpret the Will.

- Consult with a lawyer and arrange probate (court validation) of the Will.

- Help with funeral arrangements if necessary.

- Locate and deal with beneficiaries named in the Will.

- Prepare an inventory of the deceased's assets and liabilities.

- Deal with financial institutions and contacts – including banks, insurance companies and pension plans.

- Distribute assets as specified in the Will. This may involve selling real estate or other property if cash bequests are specified.

- Pay debts and estate expenses.

- Place advertisements to find creditors.

- Apply for the Canada Pension Plan benefits.

- File the deceased's final income tax returns.

Some of these tasks require financial skills, people skills and general knowledge as to what professional help is needed to provide the necessary advice to carry out these functions. Therefore the executor is allowed to hire the necessary professional help without the permission of the family or beneficiaries in most Provinces. The monies that the executor receives pay for these services. The provincial laws allow the executor to charge for their services and the amount they receive is generally based on the value of the estate.

Who Should You Consider Selecting as an Executor?

- A trusted family member

- A friend

- A non family member

- Your personal lawyer

- A Trust Company

- Your Financial Advisor

It is important that the person you chose has the predominant skills in both written and oral communication. They require these skills in order to deal with not only the family members, and beneficiaries, but with all of the business affairs that will arise. A noteworthy point to draw to your attention is that it would be best if your chosen executor did not live out of town as considerable travel and expenses could result. Gas, time, and involved duties in the carrying out of your business could be charged back to your estate. Also, with the executor being from out of town, he/she may not be familiar with your family members and business contacts.

Unfortunately there are times that family conflicts evolve and again there could be the inconvenience of increased travel and time for the executor. Not only is this inconvenient, but it could be costly in the estate process.

If an estate were complex, someone from a Trust Company would be the best choice. Before the person setting up his Will goes to that extent, it would be prudent to have the person you wish to act as your executor meet with your Financial Advisor. All three parties will then be knowledgeable as to how you wish to set up the distribution of your estate as well as to how the Financial Advisor will set up or invest those funds in order to maximize the returns until the time of distribution.

It is essential that your executor have the knowledge as to where all of your financial records are kept, and he needs to be comfortable in his own mind as to how your wish him to deal with them. This is why it may be wise to have an executive guide information list that will lay out step by step everything that will be required. That list should not only include where all of your information is kept, but all of your wishes. **Do not assume anything**. Have everything documented in black and white. It will take the guesswork out and will make the executor's job much easier.

If there is not an executor's guide in place, you may risk the chance of having your assets, bank accounts, RRSP'S, insurance policies etc. end up on the Bank of Canada's" unclaimed accounts". This could make you roll over in your grave. I know that I certainly would if I was aware that ones I wished to share my assets with, would not receive them all because the 'what and where' of my assets were not known to my executor.

I have added a list to use as a guide as to what items your executor may require in executing your Will. Once your list is completed and your family told that it exists and where it is being kept, it should be updated at least once a year.

<u>Important Documents Needed for Your Executor</u>

- Your marriage certificate (if applicable)

- Your birth certificate and that of your spouse. If you have children under the age of 25, you will also need their birth certificates as well

- The death certificate

- You social insurance number and that of your spouse

- Any divorce or separation documents; any pre-nuptial or post-nuptial agreements

- Naturalization papers (if applicable) and passports

- List of any credit cards in separate or joint names

- Burial plans, cemetery deeds

- Safety deposit box location and keys

- List of most recent statements for any chequing and saving accounts either in separate or in joint names

- The Last Will and Testament document

- A list of debts along with the most recent mortgage statement (if applicable)

- A note of any money owing to the deceased person

- Most recent tax returns

- A list of insurance policies (Health, Life, House, Tenant, Car) with the numbers of such policies

- Military Service records (if applicable)

- Auto registration or Lease agreement

- Recent statement of mutual funds, securities, stock ... in separate or joint names

- Any property deeds, partnerships or trust agreements

Note ... This information was copied from a booklet given to me by St. Joseph's Health Care London, Ontario and used with permission.

"What Needs to be Done When a Loved One Dies"

Worksheet for Executor

You will need the actual name of the Law Firm to be used by the family, complete with the full name of the lawyer, including the address, the phone number and the email address if available.

N.B. Be aware that all "powers of attorney" both for personal care and for property/finances, cease at the time of your death. At this time, the will officially takes effect and your wishes will become the active documents.

Location of Important Papers

1. Will

2. Deed to your home/cottage/other properties

3. Legal proof of age or birth certificate

4. Bill of sale or title to vehicle(s)

5. Marriage license

6. Certificate of ownership of cemetery lot, crypt or niche

7. Life insurance policies

8. Details of funeral arrangements

9. Accident and health policies

10. Tax returns, cancelled cheques and receipts for donations

11. Property damage insurance

12. Citizenship papers ... if naturalized

13. Stock certificates, bonds etc.

14. Military discharge papers

15. Copy of mortgage or lease

16. Other important documents or valuables

87 Things That Must Be Done When a Death Occurs in a Family

Indicates details that can be planned or paid ahead of time.

A) Secure Vital Statistics
*1   Name, home address and telephone number
*2   How long at present address
*3   Name of business or employer's address and telephone no
*4. Occupation and title
 5. Social Insurance Number
*6   Military Service Serial Number
*7. Date of Birth
*8. Place of Birth
*9. Citizenship
*10. Father's name
*11. Father's birthplace
*12. Mother's maiden name
*13. Mother's birthplace
*14. Religious name (if any)

B) Pay for
*15. Cemetery property
*16. Memorials
*17. Funeral arrangements
*18. Interment Service
 19. Clergy
 20. Florist
 21. Clothing
 22. Transportation
 23. Telephone and telegraph
 24.   Food and accommodation
 25.   Doctors
 26.   Nurses
 27.   Hospitals and ambulance
 28.   Medicine and drugs
 29.   Other current and urgent bills (mortgage or rent taxes. installment payments)

C) Collect Documents (Required to establish rights for insurance, pensions, social security, ownership, etc.)

*30. Will
*31. Legal proof of age or birth certificate
*32. Social Insurance number
*33. Marriage license
*34. Citizenship papers
*35. Insurance policies (life, health, automobile, property)
*36. Bankbooks
*37. Deeds to property
*38. Bill of sale of car
*39. Income tax returns, receipts or cancelled cheques
*40. Military discharge certificate
*4I. Disability claims
*42. Cemetery Certificate of Ownership

D) Decide and Arrange within a Few Hours

*43. Cemetery lot location and which space to open
*44. Memorial type and inscription
*45. Casket type
*46. Clothing for deceased
*47. Vault or sectional crypt
*48. Type of service (religious, military, fraternal)
*49. Special selection from scriptures
 50. Clergy to officiate
*51. Which funeral home
*52. Place where service to be held
 53. Time of funeral service
*54. Decide name of charitable organization(S) to which donations are suggested in memory of deceased
*55. Providing information for eulogy
*56. Select pall-bearers
 57. Flowers
 58. Music
 59. Clothing for you and children
 60. Preparation at home, including food for family and guests
 61. Extra chairs
 62. Transportation for family and guests, including planning funeral car list
 63. Checking and signing necessary papers for burial permit
 64. Providing vital statistics about deceased to newspaper
 65. Providing addresses and telephone numbers for all interested people
 66. Answering sympathetic phone calls, messages, Wires and letters

67. Meeting and talking with funeral director, cemetery representative, clergy, about details
68. Greeting friends and relatives who call
69. Arranging for meeting relatives who arrive from out of town
70. Providing lodging for out-of-town relatives
71. Make list of callers and floral tributes for mailing cards of thanks
72. Arranging for special religious services
73. Check-Will regarding special wishes
74. Order death certificate
75. Look after minor children

E) Notify as soon as possible

76. The doctor
77. The funeral director
78. The cemetery
79. Relatives
80. Friends
81. Employer of deceased
82. Employers of relatives not going to work
83. Pallbearers
84. Insurance agents (Life, Health & Accident)
85. Religious, fraternal, civic, veterans organizations, unions
86. Newspapers regarding notices
87. Lawyer, accountant and executor

The Person or Persons Most Likely Responsible for Carrying out Final Arrangements

NAME _____ Relationship_____

Address _____Tel. No. _____

NAME _____ Relationship_____

Address _____Tel. No._____

NAME_____ Relationship _____

Address _____ Tel. No._____

NAME _____Relationship_____

Address_____ Tel. No._____

To Whoever Takes the Responsibility for Final Arrangements

In calm recognition of the inevitable, we have given thought to our personal wishes concerning the final arrangements each of us desires. We feel that doing this now will minimize the emotional strain, which will come upon whichever of us survives the other. Left alone, either of us would be burdened by the great pressure of decisions on unfamiliar matters, which must be attended to immediately. Difficult as it has been for us to do this, we feel that a greater distress would be faced by one of us, or by our family and friends, if these decisions were left to be made with no indication of our specific wishes. Although these wishes may not be legally binding we hope that they will help to avoid confusion, extra expense, or at least self-reproach which might arise because of doubts, omissions, or commissions.

_____   _____
Signature   **Signature**

_____
Date

Asset Chart

TYPE	CURRENT VALUE	LOCATION

Registered Plans

RRSPs_____

Employer Pension Plan_____

Profit Sharing Plan_____

RRIFs_____

Non Registered Plans

Bank Accounts_____

Term Deposits_____

Canada Savings Bonds_____

Money Market_____

Treasury Bills_____

Foreign Currency Acc'ts_____

Other_____

Income Securities

Bonds_____

Mortgage-backed Securities_____

Income Funds_____

GICs_____

Preferred Shares_____

Income Trusts and REITs_____

Other_____

Growth Securities

Stocks_____

Equity Funds_____

Gold & Silver Certificates_____

Exchange-traded funds_____

Balanced Funds Non-registered (liquid)

Principal Residence deed_____

Recreational Property deed_____

Income Property deed_____

Limited Partnerships_____

Business Interests _____

Collectibles & Antiques_____

Jewelry, Art & Silver_____

Insurance Policies_____

Vehicle Ownership Papers_____

Insurance

Life Insurance

Company _____ Policy No _____ Amount _____

Phone Number _____ Primary Beneficiary _____

Double Indemnity __ Yes __No   Waiver of Premium __Yes __No

Company _____ Policy No. _____ Amount _____

Phone Number _____ Primary Beneficiary _____

Double Indemnity __ Yes __No   Waiver of Premium __Yes __No

Disability Income

Company _____ Policy No. _____ Amount _____

Phone Number _____ Primary Beneficiary _____

Company _____ Policy No. _____ Amount _____

Phone Number _____ Primary _____ Beneficiary _____

Health

Company _____ Policy No. _____ Amount _____

Phone Number _____ Primary _____ Beneficiary _____

Automobile

Company	Policy No	Amount

Phone Number	Primary	Beneficiary

Money on Deposit and Other Investments
(With Banks or Trust Companies)

NAME AND ADDRESS OF FINANCIAL INSTITUTION: _____

_____

Location of Deposit Books, Cheque Books and Statements: _____

_____

Type and Number of Account (Chequing, Savings, etc.) _____

_____

NAME AND ADDRESS OF FINANCIAL INSTITUTION: _____

Location of Deposit Books, Cheque Books and Statements: _____

_____

Type and Number of Account (Chequing, Savings, etc.) _____

_____

NAME AND ADDRESS OF FINANCIAL INSTITUTION: _____

Location of Deposit Books, Cheque Books and Statements: _____

_____

Type and Number of Account (Chequing, Savings, etc.) _____

_____

Safety Deposit Boxes

LOCATED AT: _____

Names and Addresses of Persons Familiar with Location of Keys to the Safety Deposit Box:

_____

LOCATED AT: _____

Names and Addresses of Persons Familiar with Location of Keys to the Safety Deposit Box:

_____

Investment Information

Credit Cards

Name of Credit Card Issuer: _____

Expiry Date: _____

Name of Credit Card Issuer:_____

Expiry Date: _____

Name of Credit Card Issuer: _____

Expiry Date: _____

Name of Credit Card Issuer: _____

Expiry Date: _____

Name of Credit Card Issuer: _____

Expiry Date: _____

Name of Credit Card Issuer: _____

Expiry Date: _____

Stocks, Bonds, GIC'S, Mutual Funds, RSP'S

Investment _____

_____
Held By   Plan/Certificate No.

Investment _____

_____
Held By   Plan/Certificate No.

Investment _____

_____
Held By   Plan/Certificate No.

Investment _____

_____
Held By   Plan/Certificate No.

Investment _____

_____
Held By   Plan/Certificate No.

Investment _____

_____
Held By   Plan/Certificate No.

_____
Financial Advisor   Business Telephone

Real Estate Investments
(Property, Business, Investment Property)

Type of Property _____   Purchase Date_____

Address/Location _____

_____
Name and Address of Mortgagor

Type of Property _____   Purchase Date_____

Address/Location _____

_____
Name and Address of Mortgagor

Type of Property _____   Purchase Date_____

Address/Location _____

_____
Name and Address of Mortgagor

Company Pensions

RETIRED   EMPLOYEE: _____   Employer: _____

Financial Institution:_____   Policy/Plan No._____

Primary and Contingent Beneficiary: _____

Monthly Amount Payable: _____   Special Provision:_____

ACTIVE EMPLOYEE: _____   Employer: _____

Insurer: _____   Policy No:_____

Primary and Contingent Beneficiary: _____

Wills and Power of Attorney

A Will is a written document giving instructions for the disposition of your property after death and appoints a personal representative, called an executor to deal with the property on your behalf. A properly drawn up-to-date Will, is one of the finest protections you can give your family.

Your lawyer will be able to assist you in drafting a Will to reflect your wishes. In addition, he or she will answer your questions regarding the executor and probate.

It is advisable that everyone should have a Will in order to have control over the distribution of his or her property. In the absence of a Will, application must be made to the court to appoint an administrator to fulfill the duties that would otherwise be carried out by an executor. The administrator appointed by the court may not be a person whom the deceased would have chosen. This then is one of the first reasons why a Will is so vital...so that you may choose your executor who will administer your estate. Discuss it with the person you plan to name as Executor; find out if he or she is willing to serve. Then discuss it with your lawyer. After you have made your Will, take your executor into your confidence regarding your wishes.

It is also advisable that a qualified person be appointed as Power of Attorney who is not necessarily your executor. This appointment gives that person the right to make decisions on your behalf should you become incompetent.

Remember that having a Will and appointing a Power of Attorney is an expression of concern for the well being of those you love. I urge you to see your lawyer as soon as possible about this.

<u>Important Facts About My Will</u>

Name: _____ My Latest will

Dated:_____

is deposited with: _____

Address: _____

The Executor of my Will is: _____ Tel. No: _____

My Power of Attorney is: _____ Tel. No:_____

The Lawyer who drew the Will is:_____

Whose address is: _____

Before you start down the tedious road of handling all the affairs of your loved one … your spouse, your partner-in-life, your soul-mate … as the executor of your loved one's affairs, I want to take a moment to look at some of the brighter moments of life.

I want to take a look at understanding some of life's trials and tribulations and generally look at your life from a past, present, and future perspective. With this in mind, I suggest you might take a few moments to read, digest and hopefully find some inner peace and tranquility for your spirit to help lift your heavy heart.

Your "happiness" has left you, much like an empty bottle floating on the whims of the ocean, with no specific time or port or destination. Please know that time is a great healer and happiness will one day return and your life will begin to re-connect and special moments will once again have meaning.

The one person who meant so much to your life, the one who cared so much about you, who took care of you, the one who stayed close to you no matter what; you must believe that their spirit still lives within you … now and always. They are in your mind and in your heart and you need only take a moment and think of them, and their image and your shared moments will appear. I discovered the following writing on the Internet and do not know the author, but I wanted to share it with you at this time.

People Come Into Our Lives for a Reason

People come into our lives for a reason, a season or a lifetime. When you know which one it is, you will know what to do for that person. When someone is in your life for a **REASON,** it is usually to meet a need you have expressed. They have come to assist you through a difficulty, to provide you with guidance and support, to aid you physically, emotionally or spiritually. That may seem like a Godsend, and they are. They are there for the reason you need them to be. Then, without any wrongdoing on your part, or at any inconvenient time, this person will say or do something to bring the relationship to an end.

Sometimes they die, sometimes they walk away, and sometimes they force you to take a stand. What we must realize is that your need has been met, your desire has been fulfilled. Their work is done. The prayer you sent has been answered and now it is time to move on.

Some people come into our lives for a **SEASON**, because your turn has come to share, to grow or to learn. They bring you an experience, or peace, or make you laugh. They may teach you something you have never done. They usually give you an unbelievable amount of joy. Believe it! It is real, but only for a **SEASON**.

LIFETIME relationships teach you lifetime lessons; things you must build upon in order to have a solid emotional foundation. Your job is to accept the lesson, love the person and put what you have learned to use in all other relationships and areas of your life.

It is often said that "Love is blind" ... but "Friendship is clairvoyant". Thank you for being part of my life whether you were there for a "reason" a "season" or a "lifetime".

True love is neither physical nor romantic. True love is an acceptance of all that is, has been, will be and will not be. Oh, by the way, peace is seeing a sunset and knowing how to be thankful. The happiest people don't necessarily have the best of everything; they just make the best of everything they have.

Many people surround you with love and care at this particular time in your life. When my soul mate died, someone cared enough to send me this poem. It has touched me so much that I felt compelled to put it in this book and share its wisdom with you.

"I wish you enough sun to keep your attitude bright.

I wish you enough rain to appreciate the sun more.

I wish you enough happiness to keep your spirit alive.

I wish you enough pain so that the smallest joys in life appear much

 bigger.

I wish you enough gain to satisfy your wanting.

I wish you enough loss to appreciate all that you possess.

I wish you enough 'hellos' to get you through the final good-bye."

...... Author unknown ......

The following four poems reflect the essence that you no doubt shared with your partner-in-life and in reality, they speak about what life really is. I have chosen a specific order to personally reflect my relationship with my own soul mate.

LOVE

FAITH

HOPE

PEACE

Love

It was a busy morning about 8:30, when an elderly gentleman in his 80's arrived to have stitches removed from his thumb. He said he was in a hurry, because he had an appointment at 9:00 a.m.

I took his vital signs and had him take a seat, knowing it would be over an hour before someone would be able to see him. I saw him looking at his watch and decided, since I was not busy with another patient, I would evaluate his wound.

On examination, it was well healed, so I talked to one of the doctors, got the needed supplies to remove his sutures and redress his wound. While taking care of his wound, I asked him if he had another doctor's appointment this morning, as he was in such a hurry.

The gentleman told me "no". He needed to go to the nursing home to eat breakfast with his wife. I inquired as to her health. He told me that she had been there for a while and that she was a victim of Alzheimer's disease.

As we talked, I asked if she would be upset if he was a bit late. He replied that she no longer knew who he was; that she had not recognized him in five years now.

I was surprised and asked him, "And you still go every morning, even though she doesn't know who you are?" He smiled as he patted my hand and said, "She doesn't know me; but I still know who she is." I had to hold back tears as he left. I had goose bumps on my arms and thought … "That is the kind of love I want in my life!"

True love is neither physical nor romantic. True love is an acceptance of all that is, has been, will be and will not be. Oh, by the way, people don't necessarily have the best of everything; they just make the best of everything they have.

Faith

God Said "No"

I asked God to take away my habit.
God said "No. It is not for me to take away, but for you to give it up."
I asked God to make my handicapped child whole.
God said "No. His spirit is whole, his body is only temporary."

I asked God to grant me patience.
God said "No. Patience is a byproduct of tribulations.
It isn't granted, it is learned."

I asked God to give me happiness.
God said "No. I give you blessings, happiness is up to you."

I asked God to spare me pain.
God said "No. Suffering draws you apart from worldly cares
and brings you closer to me."

I asked God to make my spirit grow.
God said "No. You must grow on your own,
but I will prune you to make you fruitful."

I asked God for all things that I might enjoy life.
God said "No. I will give you life so that you may enjoy all things."
I asked God to help me LOVE others as much as He loves me.
God said, "Ahhhh. Finally you have the idea."

This day is yours! Don't throw it away.

Hope

The Holy Alphabet

Although things are not perfect

Because of trial or pain,

Continue in thanksgiving.

Do not begin to blame,

Even when times are hard.

Fierce winds are bound to blow.

God is forever able.

Hold on to what you know.

Imagine life without His love.

Joy would cease to be.

Keep thanking Him for all the things

Love imparts to thee.

Move out of "Camp Complaining".

No weapon that is known

On earth can yield the power

Praise can do alone.

Quit looking at the future.

Redeem the time at hand.

Start every day with worship.

To "thank" is a command,

Until we see Him coming.

Victorious in the sky.

We'll run the race with gratitude,

Xalting God most high.

Yes, there'll be good times and yes, some will be bad, but …

Zion waits in glory … where none are ever sad!

Peace

What if tomorrow starts without me, and I'm not there to see,
If the sun should rise and find your eyes all filled with tears for me?
I wish so much you wouldn't cry, the way you did today,
While thinking of the many things we didn't get to say.
I know how much you love me ... as much as I love you,
And each time that you think of me, I know you'll miss me too.

But when tomorrow starts without me, please try to understand
that an angel came and called my name and took me by the hand,
and said my place was ready, in heaven far above
and that I'd have to leave behind, all those I dearly love.

But as I turned to walk away, a tear fell from my eye.
For all my life, I'd always thought I didn't want to die.
I had so much to live for, so much left yet to do.
It seemed almost impossible, that I was leaving you.

I thought of all the yesterdays ... the good ones and the bad.
I thought of all that we had shared and all the fun we had.
If I could relive yesterday ... just even for a while,
I'd say good-bye and kiss you and maybe see you smile.

But then I fully realized that this could never be,
For emptiness and memories would take the place of me.
And when I thought of worldly things I might miss, come tomorrow.
I thought of you and when I did, my heart was filled with sorrow.

But when I walked through heaven's gates, I felt so much at home.
When God looked down and smiled at me, from His great golden throne,
He said, "This is eternity and all I've promised you.

Today your life on earth is past; but here life starts anew.
I promise no tomorrow, but today will always last.
And since each day is the same way, there's no longing for the past."

So when tomorrow starts without me, don't think we're far apart,
For every time you think of me, I'm right here, in your heart.

General Information

Now let's get back to the business at hand. Always be aware that the people and agencies that you will have to deal with as you handle the affairs of your spouse, will not always be "gentle" and "caring" for the most part.

Although you are wearing your emotions on your sleeve, try to guard them the best way you can, as you go through the process of handing these items, remembering that to them, you are "just a number" in the myriad of calls that they have every day.

Let me enlighten you about some of the Federal, Provincial and other places that may request information about the death of a spouse. In fact, there are certain institutions that you are **required** to inform, when a spouse dies.

Where applicable, I will tell you the organization and the paperwork that is required and will even give you a sample letter as a guide **only**, to assist you in this matter.

Toll Free Helpful Numbers

Canada Pension and Old Age Security	1-800-277-9914
Goods and Services Credit	1-800-959-1953
Tax Inquiries	1-800-959-8281
Birth, Marriage and Death Certificates	1-800-461-2156
Ministry of Transportation	1-800-268-4686
Department of Veterans Affairs	1-800-668-5305
Department of Veterans Allowances	1-800-387-0919
Bell Telephone	310-2355
Rogers Telephone	1-800-980-5464
Rogers Cable	1-877-764-3722
Canada Post Corporation	1-800-267-1177
Canada Life and Health Insurance Co.	1-800-268-8099
Lawyer Referral Service	1-800-268-8326
Real Estate Council of Canada	1-800-245-6910
United States Social Security Benefits	1-313-226-6872

To Cancel Credit Cards

Gas Cards
- Petro Canada   1-800-233-8557
- Shell Canada   1-800-263-2263
- Sunoco   1-877-645-2017
- Royal Bank Visa Esso Card   1-800-769-2512

Miscellaneous Cards
- Sears   1-800-265-3675 ext. 5159
- The Bay   1-800-263-2599
- Zellers   1-800-387-4540
- Canadian Tire   1-800-263-0471
- Costco   1-800-463-3783
- Sams Club / Walmart   1-800-328-0402

Master Cards
- City Bank   1-800-387-1616
- Bank of Montreal   1-800-263-2263
- PC Financial   1-888-872-4724
- Hepcoe Mastercard (MBNA)   1-888-876-6262

Visa Cards
- Scotia Bank   1-800-387-6510
- CIBC   1-800-465-4653
- Royal Bank   1-800-769-2512
- TD Canada Trust   1-800-983-8472
- Laurentian Bank   1-800-522-1846

American Express   1-800-387-6510
- American Express Platinum Card   1-800-263-1616

Other Cards
- 407 ETR   1-888-407- 0407
- Canadian Automobile Club (CAA)   1-800-268-3750
- Air Miles   1-888-247-6453
- HBC Rewards   1-800-844-8131
- Shoppers Drug Mart   1-800-746-7737

Telephone Numbers and Addresses
Readily Accessible When a Death Occurs

The London Free Press (Classified Section)	519 – 679 – 6666
Revenue Canada	519 – 645 – 4560
London Region Ministry of Heath 217 York Street LONDON, ON N6A 5P9	519 – 675 – 6700
Canada Pension Plan Survivor Benefits Human Resources Development Canada 457 Richmond Street LONDON, ON N6A 3E3	1 – 800 – 277 – 9914
Master Card	1 – 800 – 307 – 7309
VISA	1 – 800 – 847 – 2911
Ministry of Transportation 659 Exeter Road LONDON, ON N6E 1L3	519 – 873 – 4100
London Life Insurance Company 255 Dufferin Avenue LONDON, ON N6A 4K1	519 – 435 - 7953

Some Additional Insurance Company Numbers

Canadian Life and Health Association	1-800-268-8099
Manulife (London, ON)	(519)-679-1455
London Life	1-800-667-3733
State Farm	1-800-732-5246
Allstate	1-800-732-5246
Metlife	1-800-638-5433
Zurich	1-800-983-3279

Pension Boards

Op Trust   1-800-637-0024
1 Adelaide St. East Suite 1200,
Toronto, ON   M5C 3A7   or   1-416-681-6100

Omers   1-800-387-0813
One University Avenue, Suite 700
Toronto, ON   M5J 2P1   or   1-416-369-2444

Vetern's Affairs   1-866-522-2122

Canadian Pacific   1-888-511-7557
HR Service Centre
410 9th Avenue S.W.
Calgary, AB   T2P 4Z4

Via Rail Canada Inc   1-888-842-7245

U.S. Railroad Retirement Board   1-313-226-6221
McNamara Federal Building, Suite 1199
477 W. Michigan Avenue
Detroit, MI   48226 – 2596
U.S.A.

Please note that when you are dealing with **ANY** Government office, or for that matter, **ANY** correspondence that you forward to "all persons" or to "all persons concerned", I recommend you keep a copy of **ALL** documents for your own records.

The next item I would like to discuss is the Ontario Health Care card. You must inform Ontario Health Care in writing, that your spouse has died. As required, you should also enclose a copy of the death certificate and include their cut up Health Care card.

An example of the letter that could be sent is on the following page.
As well I have included some sample letters that may be sent to notify other agencies of the passing of a loved one.

Current Date

Your Name
Your Address
Your City and Province
Your Postal Code

Ontario Health Insurance (OHIP)
217 York Street, 5th Floor
London, ON
N6A 5P9

To Whom It May Concern:

I am writing to inform you of the death of (person's name in full) on (month, day, year).

I am enclosing their OHIP card, which has been cut up, in order for your Government office to remove (person's name in full) from your file system.

I am also enclosing a copy of the death certificate for your files.

If you should require any further documentation, I may be contacted at the above address.

Thank you in advance for your prompt attention to this matter.

Sincerely,

_____

Your full name)

Current Date

Your Name
Your Address
Your City and Province
Your Postal Code

Your Phone Number (with area code)
Your email Address (if applicable)

VIA Rail Canada Inc
3 Place Ville Marie
Suite 500
Montreal Quebec
H3B 2C9

To Whom It May Concern:

I am writing to inform you of the death of (deceased's name in full) on (month, date and year).

I am enclosing his / her identification number (employee number) as well as the correct Social Insurance Number, to assist with his / her file. I am also enclosing a copy of the death certificate for your files.

I trust this information will assist you in processing my request for a lump sum Death Benefit Payment if applicable, along with the Spousal Estate Pension that may also be applicable.

If you require further information, please do not hesitate to get in touch with me at the above address.

Thank you for your prompt attention to this matter.

Sincerely

_____

Your name in full
(include your relationship to the deceased)

Current Date

Your Name
Your Address
Your City and Province
Your Postal Code

Your Phone Number (with area code)
Your email Address (if applicable)

Pension Services
HR Service Centre
Canadian Pacific
401 9th Avenue S.W.
Calgary, AB
T2P 4Z4

To Whom It May Concern:

I am writing to inform you of the death of (deceased's name in full) on (month, day, year).

I am enclosing his / her identification number (employee number), as well as the correct social insurance number, to assist you with the proper file. I am also enclosing a copy of the death certificate for your records.

I trust this information will assist you in processing my request for a lump sum Death Benefit if applicable, and with the Spousal Estate Pension that may also be applicable.

If further information is necessary, please do not hesitate to get in touch with me at the above address.

Thank you for your prompt attention to this matter.

Sincerely

_____

Your Name full name
(include your relationship to the deceased)

Federal Organizations

The first Federal organization that you should notify is the **INCOME TAX DEPARTMENT** - better known as **REVENUE CANADA.** You must make them aware of the death of your spouse and if they were receiving a "Goods and Services" rebate cheque on a quarterly basis, you must notify them.

This GST rebate cheque should no longer be sent to your spouse.

When you call Revenue Canada, they will give you another number to call as well. When you call that number, they will tell you to request certain forms: Code #**T40I1** and Code #**RC411 an**d they will forward them to your address. These forms are necessary for filing your spouse's last income tax return.

It is imperative when speaking to Revenue Canada, that you have your name put on their files as your spouse's representative in order for you to be able to access your spouse's file when it comes time to send in the return. Otherwise, Revenue Canada will seal the file and you will not be allowed access.

Also, if you were using a Chartered Accountant firm to file your return, it is imperative that their names be listed, so that they too can send and receive information on your spouse's file. Otherwise, the file will be sealed.

An example of the letter that could be sent is on the following page.

Current Date

Your Name
Your Address in full
City and Province
Your Postal Code

Winnipeg Tax Center
66 Station Road
Winnipeg, Manitoba
R3C 3M2

To Whom it may concern:

I am writing to inform you of the death of (deceased's name) on (month, day and year). I have been in touch with your office and was informed to send a letter to confirm our conversation. I have requested copies of forms: Code # T4011 and code # RC411. Plans were made to send these forms to my home address.

I was further instructed to request that I (your full name) be placed on the deceased's account as their representative because I am the Executor of the estate and the copy of the will that I am enclosing clearly states that fact. I am also enclosing a copy of (the deceased's name) death certificate as requested.

Please add our accountant's name (if applicable) to your file , so they may send and receive information as directed.

Name of Accountant or Firm
Full address including the City and Postal Code
Telephone number
Contact person.

Thank you for your prompt attention to my concerns.

Sincerely

_____

(Your name in full)

Again please let me reiterate that when you are dealing with **ANY** Government office, or for that matter, **ANY** correspondence that you forward to "all persons" or to "all persons concerned", I recommend you keep a copy of **ALL** documents for your own records.

The next item I would like to discuss is the **Social Insurance Number**. You must inform the Social Insurance Registry in writing that your spouse has died. As required, you should also enclose a copy of the death certificate and include their Social Insurance Card.

An example of the letter that could be sent is on the following page.

Current Date

Your Name
Your Address
Your City and Province
Your Postal Code

Social Insurance Registry
P.O. Box 7000
Bathurst, New Brunswick
E2A 4T1

To Whom It May Concern:

I am writing to inform you of the death of (person's name in full) on (month, date and year).

I am enclosing their Social Insurance Card, with the number (show number here). Please remove (person's name in full) from the system in your Government department.

I am also enclosing a copy of the death certificate for your files. Should you require any further documentation, please contact me at the above address.

Thank you in advance for your attention to this matter.

Sincerely

_____

(Your name in full)

Credit Cards, Interac Cards and Store Credit Cards

I was given information by my local banking establishment that I could bring in my wife's credit cards and her INTERAC card, along with a copy of the death certificate and they would look after removing my wife's name and all account information from their files.

By calling the individual companies for which my wife had credit cards, it was possible to be connected to their Business Office quite easily. For example, Sears connected me directly to their Business Office.

After speaking with the proper person and giving the reason for your call along with the deceased's full name and card number, you can discover any outstanding amount owing on a particular account. If the account shows a "nil" balance, they will close the account immediately. Consequently, you may then cut up the credit card.

All institutions must be called, but there is usually a toll-free number on the back of the credit card. They must be notified of the death, in order to close the account.

Don't forget when you are at your banking institution, you must close any separate bank accounts that your spouse has in his or her own name. The bank will usually suggest waiting a period of three months before doing this. They will want to make sure there are no outstanding transactions waiting to be conducted on the said accounts.

Safety Deposit Box

Please note: This information was taken from a booklet from St. Joseph's Health Care, London with permission... "What Needs to be Done When a Loved One Dies"

It would be very helpful if you knew the institution where the box was located and if you had the keys, as well as the box number. First of all, call the institution to see what the procedure is to be able to get into the box.

If the Safety Deposit Box is held in the name of the deceased **ONLY,** they will allow a representative of the deceased to examine the contents of the box. However, they will NOT permit the contents of said box to be removed (with the exception of the Will) **UNTIL** Letters of Probate or Letters of Administration are provided.

The Executor of the Will must get the Will probated by getting a Court Order, stating that the Will is valid and that the Executor is in fact the one named in the Will. This gives the Executor the authority to deal with the estate.

The documents that are required to deal with the estate are the following:

- An original Will
- A Petition of Letters of Probate
- An Affidavit from the Executor
- A Statement of Assets

If there is neither a Will, nor an executor named, a Letter of Administration must be ordered from the court.

Ministry of Transportation

You must inform this ministry in writing that your spouse has died. You will be required to enclose the original Driver's License in order for them to remove the deceased's name from the system. This prevents any potential future problems from arising.

An example of the letter that could be sent is as follows.

Current Date

Your Name
Your Address
Your City and Province
Your Postal Code

Ministry of Transportation
2680 Keele Street   Main Floor
Toronto, ON
M3M 3E6

To whom it May Concern:

I am writing to inform you of the death of (deceased's name in full) on (month, date and year).

I am enclosing a copy of the death certificate as well as (the deceased's name) Driver's License as required, in order that your office will delete their name and license number from your file system.

If you should require further documentation, please do not hesitate to get in touch with me at the above address.

Thank you for your prompt attention to this matter.

Sincerely

_____
Your name in full

You must not forget to contact the company that insures your vehicle. As well, you should inform them in writing that your spouse has died. If your spouse was shown as "an occasional driver", then you need simply to supply a copy of the death certificate to have the deceased's name removed from their file.

However, if your spouse had their own vehicle and subsequently, their own insurance, then it is a different story.

You will then be required to supply a copy of the Power of Attorney, which you as executor, hold. This then lets the insurance company know that you are the legal executor of the estate, and have the legal right to act as your spouse's representative. In addition, you will be required to supply a copy of the death certificate in order to facilitate the process.

Let's now turn our attention to the Pension Boards and the paperwork involved to start the process of receiving your benefits.

The first Board that I will address is the **Canada Pension Death Benefit.** The death benefit is based on how much and for how long, the deceased contributed to the Canada Pension Plan, to a maximum amount of $2,500.00. This is a one time, lump sum payment, made to the Estate of the Deceased.

IF THERE IS A WILL, the executor who is named in the Will to administer the estate, must apply for the death benefit within **60 days** of the date of death.

IF THERE IS NO WILL, and if the executor of the estate did not apply for the death benefit within 60 days of the date of death, one of the following people should apply as quickly as possible:

- The administrator appointed by the Court
- The person of Agency who has paid or who is responsible for the payment of the deceased's funeral expenses
- The surviving spouse or common-law partner of the deceased
- The next-of-kin of the deceased

Payments of the death benefit will be made in the order of priority upon application to the Canada Death Pension Benefit Board.

The second set of paperwork you must fill out and file is **The Canada Pension Plan Survivor's Pension and Child(ren)'S Benefit.**

To qualify for a "Survivor's Pension", the following conditions must apply:

- You must have been legally married or in a common-law relationship with your deceased spouse, or common-law partner at the time of the death.
- Your deceased spouse or common-law partner must have made enough contributions to the Canada Pension Plan.
- You must apply in writing and submit the necessary documentation.

If you were legally separated from your deceased spouse at the time of his/her death, you may still qualify for a Survivor's Pension.

Death Benefit
The documentation required to apply for this benefit is:

- Social Insurance Number for the deceased
- Death Certificate from the funeral home
- A Birth or Baptismal Certificate for the deceased

NOTE: If the deceased was not in receipt of the Canada Pension Plan Benefit or the Old Age Security Benefit, the Executor of the Estate must sign the application form.

Survivor Benefit

The documentation required to apply for this benefit is:

- The same documentation as above **PLUS**
- The Social Insurance number of the survivor
- A Birth or Baptismal Certificate for the survivor (if not in receipt of the Canada Pension Plan benefit or the Old Age Security benefit)
- Marriage Certificate or proof of Common-law Union

These forms are generally available at the funeral home and generally speaking, the staff of the funeral home will help with the filing of these particular forms. All you have to supply them with is the required documentation.

After the paperwork is completed the staff will even call the Canada Pension Board office and make an appointment for a specific day and time for you to go to their office. This is common practice - in other words, you do not simply walk in off the street to process the paperwork. All the paperwork and all the applications **MUST** be completed **PRIOR** to your appointment.

The location for the local Canada Pension Plan Office is as follows:

> 457 Richmond Street Suite 101
> London, ON

For an appointment, you may call 1-800-277-9914

One small item of interest that I will bring to your attention is the fact that you, as the executor/spouse, or the person named as beneficiary of the death benefit, must declare that sum of money as **income received** when you file your income tax return for the ensuing year.

The next pension board that I had to send correspondence to was that of **OP Trust,** which is a Provincial Ministry office because my spouse was an employee of the government

I informed them of my spouse's death in a written letter. I requested that I receive a spousal pension percentage, which is set out in the Ministry benefits package. Because she was a government employee, there is a $2,000.00 death benefit, according to the insurance policy held by all ministry employees. But you have to **ASK** for this, because they don't volunteer any financial assistance without a request.

If your spouse already had cheques deposited directly into your joint bank account, it would be wise to include that information and ask that it be continued. OP Trust will be looking for some form of direction for depositing the said cheque. Otherwise, they will require a new bank account number and a copy of a void cheque on that account.

Along with my letter requesting the death benefit, I included a copy of my spouse's death certificate, and a personal letter from a clergyman who stated that he knew we were living in a common-law relationship. Also in this instance, I included a copy of a void cheque from our joint bank account.

An example of the letter that could be sent is as follows.

Current date

Your Name
Your Address
Your City and Province
Your Postal Code

OP Trust
1 Adelaide Street East Suite 1200
Toronto, ON
M5C 3A7

Spouse's Name

Spouse's Social Insurance Number

Dear Sir or Madam,

I am writing to advise you of the death of my spouse (Name in full) on (day, month and year). I understand that as a spouse, I am entitled to a percentage of the existing pension.

Therefore, I am requesting the designated percentage of the existing pension to be deposited as usual, in the bank account that is already set up. I am enclosing a copy of a void cheque from that account for this purpose.

Also, I am asking that the death benefit of $2,000.00 also be deposited to the same bank account.

If there are further questions, please do not hesitate to contact me at the above address, or by telephone (your telephone number, including area code).

Thank you for your prompt attention to this matter.

Sincerely

_____
Your name in full

Current date

Your Name
Your Address
Your City and Province
Your Postal code

OMERS
1 University Avenue
Suite 700
Toronto, ON
M5J 2P1
(fax) 416-369-9704

Your Spouse's name in full
Your Spouse's Social Insurance Number

Dear Sir or Madam,

I am writing to advise you of the death of my spouse (name in full) on (day, month and year). As the spouse, I understand I am entitled to a percentage of the existing pension being paid to my spouse.

Therefore I am requesting the designated percentage of the existing pension to be deposited as usual, to the bank account that is already in existence. I am enclosing a copy of a void cheque from that account for your benefit.

I am also enclosing a copy of my spouse's death certificate for your records. If there are further questions, please do not hesitate to get in touch with me at the above address, or by telephone (your telephone number in full, including the area code).

Thank you for your prompt attention to this matter.

Sincerely

_____

Your name in full

Current Date

Your Name
Your Address
Your City and Province
Your Postal Code
Canada

Your Phone Number (with area code)
Your email Address (if applicable)

Department of the Treasury
Internal Revenue Service
Austin, TX   73301 – 0038
U.S.A.

To Whom It May Concern:

I wish to file an income tax return for (deceased's name in full) with your office because (he / she) died on (month, day, year).

Please forward a form 1310 and I shall return it, along with a copy of the death certificate for your files.

Thank you for your prompt attention to this matter.

Sincerely

_____
Your Name in Full
(Include your relationship to the deceased)

Current Date

Your Name
Your Address
Your City and Province
Your Postal Code
Canada

Your Phone Number (include area code)
Your email Address (If applicable)

U.S. Railroad Retirement Board
McNamara Federal Building
Suite 1199
477 W. Michigan Avenue
Detroit MI   48226 – 2596
U.S.A.

To Whom It May Concern:

I am writing to inform you of the death of (deceased's name in full) on (day, month and year).

I am enclosing his / her identification number (employee number), to assist you with the correct file. I am also enclosing a copy of the death certificate for your files.

I trust this information will assist you in processing my request for a lump sum Death Benefit if applicable, and with the Spousal Estate Pension that may also be applicable.

If further correspondence is needed, please do not hesitate to get in touch with me at the above address.

Thank you for your prompt attention to this matter.

Sincerely

_____

Your name in full
(include your relationship to the deceased)

United States Railroad Retirement Board
844 North Rush Street
CHICAGO, Illinois 60611 – 2092
http://www.rrb.gov

N.B. The information provided below comes from their Handbook 1B-2. dated February 2007.

The Railroad Retirement Board's mission is to administer retirement / survivor and unemployment / sickness insurance benefit programs for railroad workers and their families, under the Railroad Retirement Act and the Railroad Unemployment Insurance Act. These programs provide income protection during old age and in the event of disability, death or temporary unemployment and sickness.

The Railroad Retirement Act is a federal law that provides retirement and disability annuities for qualified railroad employees, spouse annuities for their wives or husbands and survivor benefits for the families of deceased employees who were insured under the act.

In addition, a "toll-free" help line is available at 1-800-808-0772. This number can be used to obtain the addresses and telephone numbers of any of the Board's field offices.

Survivor Benefits

Annuities are payable to surviving widows' and widowers' children and certain other dependents. Lump sum benefits are payable after the death of a railroad employee, only if there are no qualified survivors of the employee who are immediately eligible for monthly annuities. With the exception of a residual lump-sum death benefit, eligibility for survivor benefits depends on whether or not the employee was "insured" under the Railroad Retirement Act at the time of death.

An employee is insured if he or she has at least **10 years** of railroad service, or **5 years'** service performed after 1995 and has a current connection with the Railroad industry, as of the month the annuity begins, or the month of death, which ever occurs first.

Current Connection Requirement

An employee who worked for a Railroad for at least 12 months in the 30 months immediately preceding the month his or her Railroad Retirement Annuity begins, will meet the current "connection" requirement for a supplemental annuity, occupational disability annuity, or the survivor benefits described later.

(If the employee dies before retirement, railroad service for at least 12 months in the 30 months before the month of death, will meet the current "connection" requirement for the purpose of paying survivor benefits.)

If an employee does not qualify on this basis, but has 12 months' service in an earlier 30 month period, he or she may still meet the current "connection" requirement.

Types of Survivor Benefits

Annuities are payable to widows, widowers and unmarried children. In certain cases, benefits are also payable to parents, remarried widow or widower, grandchildren and surviving, and divorced spouses.

Survivor Annuities may also be payable to a surviving, divorced spouse, or remarried widow or widower. Benefits are limited to the amount that Social Security would pay and therefore are less than the amount of the Survivor Annuity which would otherwise be payable.

However, effective August 17, 2007, Tier II Benefits may be extended to surviving former spouses, pursuant to Divorce agreements.

Other survivor annuities are payable to:

- An unmarried child under age 18

- An unmarried child, age 18 in full-time attendance at an elementary or secondary school, or in approved "home schooling", until the student attains the age of 19, or the end of the school term in progress, when the student attains the age of 19

- An unmarried, disabled child over the age of 18, if the child became totally and permanently disabled before the age of 22

- An unmarried dependent grandchild, meeting any of the requirements described above for a child, if both the grandchild's parents are deceased or disabled

- A parent at the age of 60, who was dependent on the employee for at least half of the parent's support, if the employee was also survived by a widow or widower, a surviving divorced spouse or child, who could ever qualify for an annuity. The parent's annuity is limited to the amount that Social Security would pay.

Survivor Annuity Estimates

The best way for survivors to obtain an annuity estimate is to visit or telephone the nearest Board Field Office. Active or retired employees, who are concerned about the amount of benefit which would be payable to their survivors, may also receive estimates from the nearest Board Field Office.

The following information may be helpful in providing an idea of the potential amount of survivor benefits. The average annuity awarded to a widow or widower in the fiscal year 2006, excluding remarried widow or widower and surviving, divorced spouses was $1,489 a month. On the average, children received $1,056 a month. Total family benefits for widow or widower with children, averaged $2,989 a month. The average annuity awarded to remarried widow or widower or surviving divorced spouses in 2006 was $831 a month.

Survivor Annuity Tiers

Survivor annuities, like Retirement annuities, consist of Tier I and Tier II components.

TIER I

This is based on the deceased employee's combined Railroad Retirement and Social Security credits and is generally equivalent to the amount that would have been payable under Social Security.

TIER II

This amount is based on percentages of the deceased employee's Tier II amount, as described in the section on formula at the back of the pamphlet called **IB – 2** and dated February 2007.

When Survivor Payments Stop

All survivor payments stop upon death and no annuity is payable for the month during which the death occurred.

A widow's annuity will be reduced upon remarriage and in some cases payments will be prevented. A widow's surviving, divorced spouses' and remarried widow's annuity could also end, upon entitlement to another survivor or spouse annuity, under the Railroad Retirement Act, which is greater than the widow's annuity.

A surviving, divorced spouse's or remarried widow's annuity could stop, when entitled to a Social Security Benefit, which equals or exceeds the deceased employee's basic Tier I amount and reduces the annuity amount to zero.

Lump - Sum Death Benefits

A lump-sum death benefit is payable to certain survivors of an employee with 10 or more years of Railroad service, or less than 10 years, if at least 5 years were after 1995 and the employee had a current connection with the Railroad industry, if there is no survivor immediately eligible for a monthly annuity, upon the employee's death.

The amount payable depends primarily on whether the deceased employee was credited with 10 years of service before January 1, 1975. In this case the average benefit payable is about $900. In all other cases, where a lump sum is payable, the benefit is $255.

Retirement and Survivor Information

Applying for an Annuity

Applications for Railroad Retirement or Survivor Benefits are generally filed at one of the Board's Field Offices, or with a traveling Board representative, at a customer outreach program service location, or by telephone and mail.

The Board accepts applications up to 3 months in advance or an annuity beginning date, which allows the agency to complete the processing of most new claims by a person's retirement date.

Also, effective for applications filed on or after January 1, 2006, an employee can be in "compensated service" while filing a Disability Application, provided that the compensated service terminates within 90 days from the date of filing.

Railroad employees can also get estimates of their future annuities over the Internet. They can access this service by visiting www.rrb.gov and clicking on "Benefit Online Service (Main Line)" for directions on establishing an RRB Internet Service Account.

Persons applying for Railroad Retirement Benefits will be automatically enrolled in the U.S. Treasury's direct deposit program, which will electronically transfer Federal payments into individual's checking or savings accounts.

However, Direct Deposit Waivers are available to individuals who state that Direct Deposit would cause a hardship and to individuals without bank accounts. Applicants for Railroad Retirement and Survivor Benefits can check with their local Board Field Office, as to when they may expect their first payment.

Customer service standards and progress reports are available in Field Offices and on line at www.rrb.gov .

To expedite filing, applicants should contact their local Board Office for a Pre-Retirement consultation

Certain documents are required when filing a Railroad Retirement Annuity application:

For Employees and Spouses

- Proof of an employee's age
- Proof of any military service
- Proof of marriage, if the spouse is eligible or will shortly become eligible for a spouse annuity. A divorced spouse must furnish proof of divorce from the employee.
- Proof of the spouse's or divorced spouse's age
- Proof of a child's relationship and age, if the spouse is applying for an annuity based on caring for the employee's child
- Notice of any Social Security benefit award, or other Social Security claim determination
- Information about any Public Service Pension for which the applicant qualifies
- Banking information for Direct Deposit of benefit payments

For Survivors

- A widow(er) **must** furnish proof of age; proof of marriage and proof of the employee's death (Death Certificate).
- A surviving, divorced spouse **must** furnish proof of divorce from the employee.

Monitoring Retirement and Survivor Benefit Payments

Under several monitoring programs now in effect, the Board maintains contact with the Retirement and Survivor Beneficiaries, in order to ensure the reporting of events, which would require suspension or termination of monthly benefits.

The records of beneficiaries are also checked with the Social Security Administration, because non-railroad earnings may affect annuities and because entitlement to Social Security benefits affects the amount of all annuities.

Service and Earnings Records

The Railroad Retirement Board maintains a record of all covered Railroad Service and Creditable earnings after 1936. The information is recorded under the employee's Social Security Account Number, used by the employer to report service and compensation to the Board.

Pre – Arranging Your Funeral

No one likes to think about his or her own funeral, but it is inevitable. If you do your homework early by putting down your wishes, and better yet, if possible, by paying your funeral expenses in advance, you do your family a great service. If nothing is in place, your family is left not only with the burden of dealing with your passing, but they may have to make some difficult decisions when their thinking process may not be clear.

By pre-arranging and paying for your funeral you may save some money for your estate. If you wish to pre-arrange your funeral, start by contacting a local funeral home. Provincial Boards or Councils license funeral homes. This license ensures that the funeral director understands all of the legislation governing funerals in the province and it also authorizes funeral home staff to sell their services in advance of a death.

The funeral director will outline various products and services that you may pre-arrange. These services may include embalming, transportation, visitation arrangements, the facilities itself, a variety of ceremonies available and a casket or urn. Your may wish to visit several funeral homes to compare services and prices.

Leaving all of these decisions to your family after your demise may make them feel pressured and due to their emotional state it may be difficult for them to make thoughtful, informed decisions.

Because you may feel a bit emotional yourself when planning your arrangements you may wish to have a family member or a close friend along for support. Once you have chosen a funeral home and the type of service you would like to have, you simply leave a record of your preferences with the funeral home and tell them that the estate will pay the costs at the time of your death.

If you wish to pre-pay, be aware that there are two types of pre-arrangements.

- Guaranteed

- Non-guaranteed

In a **guaranteed** contract, you pay a certain amount for a specified list of products and services and the funeral home guarantees that price until the date of your funeral. One of the best benefits of this option is that it "locks in" today's prices and therefore is a hedge against inflation, because the money you deposit, plus the interest accrued, is used to pay the expenses of your funeral.

Be sure to ask if the funeral home will allow you to pay for a guaranteed contract in installments. Some funeral homes will allow this but unfortunately most funeral homes will ask you to pay the entire fee in a lump sum. You should also request that the funeral home send you a yearly statement of the account they hold on your behalf.

In a **non-guaranteed** contract (sometimes called a deposit contract) you set aside money for funeral expenses either all at once or in installments.
However, the funeral home does not guarantee that the amount set aside will cover the cost at the time of your death. This type of contract is often used for expenses that are "outside" the control of the funeral home, such as flower costs, newspaper notices, and the honorarium for the clergy.

At the time of this writing, the average funeral costs in Canada include **approximately** $3,500 for funeral services, $3000 for the casket and $1,500 for a vault, plus cemetery or crematorium costs.

As with anything you purchase, e.g. a car, you can buy a Cadillac or a Volkswagen. The prices vary, as too do the prices when selecting a casket. You may purchase a simple particleboard casket for a few hundred dollars or pay thousands of dollars for a metal casket. It all depends on what you can afford and your personal preferences.

When paying for a funeral in advance the money is placed in a trust account, which is covered by the Canadian Deposit Insurance Corporation. This money **is not part** of the Funeral Homes operating costs, so even if the funeral home closes or goes bankrupt, your investment is safe.

The money that you deposit with the Trust Account also earns interest under the Income Tax Act. That interest is tax free with the knowledge that your pre-payment is $15,000.00 or less. In Ontario the funeral home must refund any excess interest to the estate.

When pre-paying for a funeral, be sure that funeral home will allow you to cancel the contract with them, and ask if the contract can be transferred to another funeral home if necessary. Also be sure you are aware of what the cancellation fees will be.

On cancellation the funeral home will issue a T5 slip, as you will be required to pay income tax on the accumulated interest.

If there is the possibility you may move to another city or province at some time, it would be prudent to deal with a funeral home that exists in that location, or one that is connected to the Canadian Independent Group of Funeral Homes that represent independently owned and operated funeral homes from across Canada.

A noteworthy point here is that re-arranging your funeral does not obligate your family or your executor to follow your requests. Either party can override your wishes after your death. Therefore it may be a good idea to discuss your funeral arrangements with your family and executor. Look for input and form a sense of congeniality so that all are in agreement with your wishes. This may be the last say you will have as to how you wish to have things done. Hopefully your family will respect all of these wishes.

Be sure that all parties have a copy of your funeral contract. Do not leave the only copy in a safety deposit box. Banks usually do not allow access to the safety deposit box until a death certificate has been issued by the funeral home. Leaving a copy of your contract with your executor and with your family members will allow for a smooth transition in making the final arrangements and in carrying out your final wishes.

When pre planning a funeral, make an itemized cost of all items and services that you have on your list of things you want to be done or items you wish to purchase. The law in many jurisdictions must make price lists made available to the public at no charge and with no obligations. Try not to be pressured by aggressive sales tactics. Once you have decided on any arrangements, be sure to receive a written contract.

In the Yellow Pages of your phone book, under "Funerals" you may find a Memorial Society. These non-profit groups help their members negotiate simple, economical funerals with Funeral homes.

If you encounter a problem or if you feel you have been treated poorly by a funeral home, do not hesitate to report this to an establishment called the " Self-Governing Board of Funeral Directors." This board oversees the industry and administers the Funeral Directors and Establishments Act, including offering recourse to dissatisfied consumers through its complaint process.

Once again, always be sure to make your wishes known to your loved ones, even if you do not pre-plan your funeral. This job will be a lot easier for them, if they know your preferences and your wishes.

Funeral -Arrangements and Special Wishes

Name:_____

Funeral Prearranged _____

Funeral Home Preferred _____

Person's Wishes:
Visitation Preferred ____Afternoon ____ Evening____ Both_____

Embalming ____Yes ____No

Open Casket ____Yes ____No

Type of Casket Wood _____ Metal _____ Cloth _____

Church Service _____Yes _____No

Funeral Home Chapel Service _____Yes _____No

Fraternal Service _____Yes _____No

Flowers _____Yes _____No   Favorites _____

Contribution in lieu of flowers _____Yes _____No

Charity/ Association _____

Eulogy By _____

Other Special Wishes (music, favorite poems etc) _____

_____

Pallbearers:

_____

_____

Cemetery Arrangements

We recognize the value of pre-planning and have made cemetery arrangements with:

Name of Cemetery _____

Address _____

City and Province _____Tel. Number_____

The items we have pre planned are:

Ground Burial

___ Cemetery Lots

___ Burial Vaults

___ Bronze Memorial

___ Granite Base

___ Upright Monument

___ Ground Opening and Closing fees

Cremation Burial

___ Cremation Lots

___ Cremation Vault/ Urn

___ Cremation Memorial

___ Cremation Lot Opening and Closing Fees

___ Cremation Fees

Mausoleum Entombment

___ Mausoleum Crypt

___ Crypt Memorial

___ Vases

___ Candles

___ Pictures

___ Crypt Entombment Fees

Cremation Niches

___ Columbarium Niche

___ Niche Urns

___ Niche Memorial

___ Niche Vase

___ Niche Opening/ Closing Fees

___ Cremation Fees

A List of Documents and Information You May Wish to Have on Hand

1. Your marriage certificate (if applicable)

2. Your birth certificate and that of your spouse. If you have children under the age of 25, you will also need their birth certificates as well.

3. The death certificate

4. Your social insurance number and that of your spouse.

5. Any divorce or separation documents; any pre-nuptial or post-nuptial agreements

6. Naturalization papers (if applicable) and passports

7. List of any credit cards in separate or joint names

8. Burial plans, cemetery deeds

9. Safety deposit box location and keys

10. List of most recent statements for any chequing and saving accounts either in separate or in joint names

11. The Last Will and Testament document

12. A list of debts along with the most recent mortgage statement (if applicable)

13. A note of any money owing to the deceased person

14. Most recent tax returns

15. A list of insurance policies (Health, Life, House, Tenant, Car) with the numbers of such policies

16. Military Service records (if applicable)

17. Auto registration or Lease agreement

18. Recent statement of mutual funds, securities, stock ... in separate or joint names

19. Any property deeds, partnerships or trust agreements

__Note__ ... *This information was copied from a booklet given to me by St. Joseph's Health Care London, Ontario and used with permission.* *"What Needs to be Done When a Loved One Dies"*

Last Will and Testament

This is the **Last Will and Testament** of me,

_____

_____ of _____ in the

Province of _____ made the _____ day of

_____ , 200_ .

I REVOKE all former Wills, Codicils, or other Testamentary Dispositions by me at

any time and declare this to be and contain my Last Will and Testament.

I APPOINT

_____

of _____ in the

Province of _____ to be Executor of

this my Last Will and Testament.

BUT IF my said Executor should refuse to act, predecease me, or die within a

period of_____ days following my death, **THEN I APPOINT**

_____

in the Province of _____ to be Executor of

this my Last Will and Testament.

I DIRECT all my just debts, funeral and testamentary expenses to be paid and

satisfied by my Executor as soon as conveniently may be after my death.

I APPOINT

_____

of _____ in the

province of_____ as Guardian(s) of my minor

children but if _____

should refuse to act ,or predecease me, or die within _____ days following

my death, **THEN I APPOINT**

_____of_____

_____ in the province _____as

Guardian(s) of my minor children.

I REQUEST that my Guardian(s):

IN WITNESS whereof I have set my hand the day and year written above.

_____
(Signature)
This page was signed and the preceding pages were initialed by the Testator and
published and declared as and for his/her last Will and Testament in the
presence of us both present together at the same time who at his/her request
and in his/her presence and in the presence of each other have hereunto
subscribed our names as witnesses.

Name: _____

Address: _____

_____

(Signature)

Name: _____

Address: _____

_____

(Signature)

I give my Executor the following **POWERS**:

_____

_____

_____

_____

_____

_____

_____

I DISTRIBUTE my assets as such:

_____

_____

_____

_____

_____

<u>Living Will</u>

This document is made with the wish that it be honored in all provinces in Canada and is meant to fulfill the legal requisite of an **Advance Health Care Directive**, **Health Care Directive**, **Personal Directive**, **Authorization to Give Medical Consent**, **Continuing Power of Attorney for Personal Care**, and **Representation Agreement for Health Care.**

To my family, my physician, my cleric, my lawyer, or any medical facility or person who may become responsible for my health, welfare or affairs, let it be known that:

This is the **Living Will and Medical Directive** of:

_____

currently residing in the Province of_____

- **I REVOKE** all former Living Wills, Personal Directives, or Advance Medical Directives given by me at any time.

- I hereby indemnify and hold harmless my Agent and anyone who acts in good faith at the request of my Agent to fulfill my wishes expressed in this document.

- **I APPOINT**

  _____

  of _____ in

  the province of _____to be my **Agent** and

  to make personal and health care decisions on my behalf if, and when, I no longer have the mental or physical capacity to make such decisions myself.

- If my appointed Agent is unwilling or unable to act on my behalf, then I appoint the first person on the following list that is able and willing to serve as my Agent.

  _____ of _____

  _____ of _____

- This directive will be in effect when, and only when, I am unable to make or communicate my own decisions by speaking, writing or gesturing.

- If my spouse has been designated as an Agent or Alternative Agent in this document and if after the making of this document my spouse and I become legally separated or divorced, any legal rights or powers granted to my spouse by this document shall be revoked.

- Any reference to Agent in this document shall also apply to an Alternative Agent.

- I grant to my Agent the absolute power and authority to make all decisions affecting my health and welfare, and request that my Agent and all to whom he/she shall give directions in these matters follow my wishes and instructions as given herein to the best of my Agent's interpretation of my wishes. In particular, but not restricted to, I grant to my Agent the power and authority to: sign documents including releases, permissions, or waivers: to review and disclose medical records: to hire and discharge Caregivers: to authorize admission to or release from medical facilities: and to consent to, refuse or withdraw consent to any form of health care.

- It is my wish that should a situation arise that there is no reasonable expectation of my recovery and I am being kept alive by artificial or mechanical means, that

_____

_____

_____

_____

_____

_____

_____

If it becomes necessary to appoint a Guardian of my person then I nominate my Agent who is appointed in this document to be my Guardian.

I declare when signing here that I am of sound mind, and that I understand the content of this document and the power it gives to my Agent, and I declare that this document represents my wishes.

Dated and signed this _____ day of _____ , 200__ in the

Province of_____

_____
(Signature)
Signed in the presence of:

Witness: (print) _____

Signature: _____

Witness: (print) _____

Signature: _____

Enduring Power of Attorney

The authority given by this power of attorney shall continue in effect notwithstanding any subsequent mental incapacity of the donor.

I_____

of _____ in the

Province of _____ state:

I REVOKE all former Enduring Powers of Attorney previously given by me.

I APPOINT

_____

of _____ in the

Province of _____ to be my attorney.

BUT IF my said attorney should refuse to act, predecease me, or die within a

period of_____ days following my death, **THEN I APPOINT**

_____ of

_____

in the Province of _____ to be my

attorney.

This Power of Attorney will be EFFECTIVE

Date: _____

The decision to activate this Power of Attorney shall be subject to the evaluation

and written declaration of_____

My attorney has the POWER TO carry out the following:

_____

_____

My attorney is RESTRICTED FROM the following:

_____

_____

My attorney shall RECEIVE PAYMENT on the following terms:

_____

_____

If this Enduring Power of Attorney is the cause of any disagreement:

_____

_____

Dated at _____ this

_____ day of _____ , 200 ____ .

_____
(Signature)

Witnessed by (print): _____

Signature of Witness: _____

Witnessed by (print): _____

Signature of Witness: _____

Worksheet for an Executor

You should have on hand, the name of the specific Funeral Home that the family wishes to use. You also need to have all paper work in place with regard to the deceased's wishes regarding burial or cremation.

You also need to be aware if a casket is to be purchased or if renting a sleeve to insert into a casket is an option. Is the casket to be open or closed? If "renting" the casket, has the person picked out the container to hold their cremated remains? Does the Executor know the cost for cremation? In 2004, the approximate cost was in the $400.00 range.

Does the Executor know the following:

- The name of the cemetery

- Whether or not the burial plot has already been purchased

- If the headstone has been discussed or purchased
  if not, then what information is to be put on the stone

- The name of the minister they want to conduct the service

- Is it to be a religious service in a church or in the funeral home?

- Is it a private service for family only or is it to be a memorial service?

- Will there be music? If so, then what kind? Are there any personal choices? Can a CD be used?

- What about flowers? What are the deceased's favorite kind?

- Is the executor responsible for paying for all the flowers from the family?

- Is there to be a hall rental afterwards for refreshments or does the Funeral Home have its own facilities and are they available?

- What kinds of refreshments are to be provided and for how many people?

For your convenience, many food stores will make platters of food available for such occasions. Catering services are also available. If you plan to do this yourself, you might include paper plates, napkins, cutlery, glassware, tea, coffee, juice, condiments etc.

- Are there to be special tributes given by one or more family members?

- Is the minister presiding or is there another person presiding over the service?

- Are there particular people acting as pall bearers; have they been asked?

- Has the clothing for the deceased been taken to the Funeral Home?

- Has there been a death notice put in the local paper?

- Are there to be memorial donations? If so, to what organization or charity?

Choosing an Executor

First let's revisit what an executor does. He/she is the estates legal representative. He/she will pay bills, taxes and divide up the assets. As a given rule, family members are usually chosen and since they are most likely beneficiaries as well they are most likely motivated to act quickly in processing your Will. By law, executors are entitled to claim compensation for their time and trouble in processing the estate. He/she can receive awards of up to 5% of your estate.

Executor's "to-do" List

When accepting this position be well aware that if an executor breaches his or her duties, or fails to protect the estate, they can be sued.

An executor's responsibilities **may** include:

- Find the original will and any codicils that amend it

- Confirm with your lawyer that the will is valid

- Secure valuables, protect the property

- Arrange for the funeral

- Notify the next of kin

- If necessary hire a lawyer if probate if required

- Prepare inventory and appraisals of the deceased's assets

- Pay all bills, taxes and debts and cancel credit cards

- Get investment, legal, business and/or tax advice

- Sell or distribute assets to beneficiaries

- Have beneficiaries approve and release you from any claims
  (**Get this in writing**)

It is almost always a good idea to have a back up executor in place for various reasons. The initial person chosen may not be able to fulfill the estates duties due to age or illness or they may resign as your executor for unknown circumstances. Be aware that if young children are involved you may need to protect their inheritance on a long-term basis. It may then be wise to appoint a younger individual as your executor. Also in this latter circumstance you might like to consider choosing multiple executors or, hire a Trust Company.

An executor may find the responsibilities too much for them to handle and may turn the handling of the estate over to another appointed executor. At this time it is best that they sign a court form. This can only be done if no work has been done on the estate. However, if work has been started on the estate then he/she will need the beneficiaries consent to resign. The executor could be held responsible for the legal cost required for court approval.

An executor does not need to sign anything to take on the job of being your executor. Also, note, he/she does not need to be a beneficiary, nor a witness to the Will. All an executor has to do is verbally consent to take on the job.

Anyone being asked to be an executor should not jump into the responsibly of taking it on without some soul searching that he/she is up to the task. They need to know they can commit to the task of investing their time and their best efforts to see the process through. After making a solid decision that they are capable of this commitment, then it is time you should seek out your lawyer to put down your thoughts for the dispersements of your assets.

Executors don't always come with experience. They should be someone you trust implicitly and they should have a handle on processing their own affairs. If the person you are thinking of appointing tells you they have a problem balancing their bankbook then you should hear bells, and realize your choice may not be a good candidate.

Your lawyer can explain how you can put in a system of checks and balances, to minimize possible abuse by someone expected to protect your estate.

Just as when you are in control of your assets, you may not have control of unforeseen events after your passing. The market could crash, there could be a fire or an accident that could destroy valuable assets, or a business could loose money. Executors could be blamed or sued for these particular loses. Make sure your Will covers these contingencies. It is wise to protect your executor by having an experienced estate lawyer include clauses in your Will to protect the executors. Otherwise, your executor may renounce their position and refuse to act.

Leaving an Estate Guidebook

Your executor needs information on where to find your will, any special instructions and your estate inventory. You cannot imagine how much time can be lost just looking for financial information or worrying about funeral arrangements. Putting your affairs in order gives your executor a road map to move ahead more efficiently.

There are a couple of remaining jobs that may need your attention as the spouse or the executor of the estate. That would be to contact any Church, Club or Organization with which your spouse was affiliated. In all likelihood, most of these would have seen the newspaper notice or heard by word of mouth that your spouse had died and consequently, members of the above may be present at the service.

As the executor/spouse, your final job is to send out cards of thanks for flowers received and for donations to charities in your spouse's memory.

You may also wish to place an ad in the local newspaper, to thank all those who were involved in the health care given, with home care assistance, thanks to friends and others who came to offer support as well as special thanks to member of the family for their support during this time of sorrow.

I have included my personal newspaper ad for two reasons:

1. Simply as an example for consideration;

2. As my final tribute to my wife Wendy, for all the love, care and devotion that I received from her for many years and of which I am now deprived.

Wendy Jane McCarthy

February 18, 1943 -May 14, 2004

I would like to express the family's gratitude for all the cards of sympathy from the family, friends and past employees from the workplace. I would also like to express my heartfelt thanks to all of those who attended both the visitation and funeral services for Wendy. I would also like to thank those who gave flowers and memorials to charities as a remembrance of Wendy. I would also like to thank the nursing staff of six (6) North Cancer Unit at the new Victoria Hospital. Their kindness and readiness for Wendy's comfort was very much present. I would especially like to thank the nursing staff on the fifth (5) floor Palliative Care Unit, Parkwood Hospital, for their very vigilant care for Wendy's ever increasing comfort level. You ladies do your nursing profession proud and put the families of the patient at ease, knowing the excellent care is always there for their family members. Last but by no means least; I would like to recognize a great Doctor by the name of Doctor John Swift. The man as a Doctor stands in a class of his own. His caring, his home visitations, his every waking hour, I'm convinced, is dedicated to all of his patients wellness and comfort. He is the only Doctor that I have seen, when in his company, give Wendy a hug when her spirit was so low. Truly you touched both Wendy's and my heart for that kindness shown. I hold you above all men, as on a scale of one to ten, you are definitely an eleven.

Thank you all and God Bless
Her husband, Paul Tolmie.

Husband's Eulogy to His Wife

Now is the hour of pain.
Its presence is eminent in our heart.
The weight of sorrow is heavy.
There seems no relief from its weight.
Time is heavy on our being,
And relief from suffering seems distant.
Hold on! Hold on to good thoughts.
Be consumed by them. Hold tight!!

There will be a tomorrow
and a day after that, and that.
Healing is a slow process.
Take pleasure in the fact that you knew her and loved her as
she knew and loved you back.
Remember her laugh, her smile, her wit.
She could lift your spirit and make you feel alive ...
or put you in line and wish you weren't.

She touched those who came into her world
and left her mark.
Our world will be none the better with her passing,
but she did leave us a piece of her ...
her daughter Laura and her son Brent.
They have her values and her ways.
They have her strengths.
They have her skills.

When one looks on them, there's our Wendy.
She is not lost to us.
She will always have our hearts.
She will always be in our minds.
She will always be in our prayers.
Life will be able to go on for us,
as she is with us now and forever.

Be at peace Wendy .You are still with us!

Author: Stephen Paul Tolmie

My Final Thoughts

I have hopefully helped to give you motivation to set pen to paper to help decide your wishes for your Estate Distribution, your Will, Power of Attorney and Power of Attorney for Personal Care. My intentions were two fold. To make you **THINK** and then to **ACT UPON YOUR WISHES** so that nothing is left to chance. This is so important not only to you but to assist your loved ones with what needs to be done, and how you wish them to go about it. It will help to show that your last thoughts were your love for them and your wishes to see them looked after when you are gone. This also eases the pain of decision making on their part as the workbook format can be followed easily. The information provided will help your family deal with your loss and in essence still put them in touch with you.

I encourage you to use this book, to help you deal with your own personal estate planning and also encourage you to use the workbook pages, as you begin to deal with the myriad of things that may become necessary to complete when a loved one dies.

If in some small way I have helped to lift the burden and stress at a most difficult time, then my time has been well spent.

I discovered a poem that I feel covers my previously mentioned comments and I would like to share it with you.

> I may never see tomorrow.
> There's no written guarantee
> And things that happen yesterday
> Belong to history.
>
> I cannot predict the future.
> I cannot change the past.
> I have just the present moment.
> I must treat it as my last.
>
> I must use the moment wisely
> For it soon will pass away
> And be lost to me forever
> As part of yesterday.
>
> I must exercise compassion.
> Help the fallen to their feet.

Be a friend to the friendless,
Make an empty life complete
The unkind things I do today
May never be undone
And friendship that I fail to win
May nevermore be won.

Author: Unknown

I would like to express that although some of this material is site specific, I deeply hope that the workbook will be helpful in providing contacts. It also provides lists of information that may be required and gives samples of the business format type letter that needs to accompany the information that you are supplying.

REMEMBER THAT ALTHOUGH THEIR BODY HAS BEEN REMOVED FROM YOU, THEIR SPIRIT WILL ALWAYS REMAIN IN YOUR HEART AND MIND UNTILL YOU ARE ONCE AGAIN REUNITED!!!

About the Author

I am attempting to assist people from my personal knowledge and research material into the subject of Estate Planning and Executor Guide. (What it means; what's involved; and its process.)

Hopefully in some small way this workbook will assist you in your estate planning or if nothing else**…"Make you stop and think…..I have to do this. No more putting it off."**

Secondly I hope it will make you aware of the responsibilities and the commitment that he/ she needs to be informed of prior to accepting the position of becoming your executor.

As they say, "Planning is the key to success", in processing all that needs to be done in order to allow for a smooth transition in processing a person's estate.

My attempt in laying out this information workbook is to enable you to see what is indeed there, what needs to be there and what amendments you want to make, before seeing a lawyer to have your requests legally documented as your Last Will and Testament.

One last item I wish to bring to light about myself is that I have written two books. The first book published was a tribute to my wife that I had lost in 2004. The book title is, **Now You Have Her… Now You Don't.** The second book was entitled, **That Single Moment**, which again deals with the loss of loved ones.

God Bless

Stephen Paul Tolmie

Printed in the United States
By Bookmasters